THAT'S REGRETTABLE

THAT'S REGRETTABLE

*Releasing the Past to
Fuel Your Future*

LEEANN MARIE WEBSTER

AVIVA
PUBLISHING

New York

That's Regrettable: Releasing the Past to Fuel Your Future

Copyright © 2025 by LeeAnn Marie Webster

Published by:

Aviva Publishing
Lake Placid, NY 12946
518-523-1320
www.avivapubs.com

Address all inquiries to:
LeeAnn Marie Webster
1953 N Clybourn #R-168
Chicago, IL 60614

All rights reserved. No part of this publication may be reproduced, distributed, or transmitted in any form or by any means, including photocopying, recording, or other electronic or mechanical methods, without the prior written permission of the publisher, except in the case of brief quotations embodied in critical reviews and certain other noncommercial uses permitted by copyright law.

Cover Design: Anže Ban Virant, ABV atelier design, https://abvatelier.com
Interior Design: Catherine Williams, Chapter One Book Design, https://chapter-one-book-production.co.uk

Library of Congress Control Number: 2025916699
ISBN: 978-1-63618-406-7

10 9 8 7 6 5 4 3 2 1

First Edition, 2025

Printed in the United States of America

This book is dedicated to every person who bravely faced their regret and shared it with me.

And to my brother Daniel who inspires me to live fully every day.

CONTENTS

Introduction	1
Regrets Related to Friends	3
Regrets Related to Career & Education	17
Regrets Related to Family	39
Regrets Related to Self	69
Regrets Related to Romantic Partners	91
Regrets Related to Money	109
Regrets Related to Health	121
Regrets Related to Miscellaneous Moments	133
Regret Rewrite	155
Acknowledgments	159

INTRODUCTION

Regret is universal. It doesn't care where you live, how much money you make, or what you believe in—it finds all of us eventually. I've spent years collecting handwritten regrets from strangers and audiences around the world. Some are funny. Some are heartbreaking. All of them are real. This book is a glimpse into those raw, honest moments—the things we wish we'd said, done, or dared—and a reminder that regret doesn't have to weigh us down forever. Once revealed, regret can be released. And when we release it, we create space for growth, healing, and bold new beginnings.

This work is personal for me. When I was just four years old, my older brother Daniel was killed in a car accident (he was twelve). Losing him so suddenly shaped how I see the world—it taught me, far too early, that tomorrow isn't promised. I believe those of us still here have a responsibility to make the most of the time we're given. That's why I do this work. That's why I collect these regrets—not to dwell in the past, but to help us all live with fewer regrets, more courage, and no limits.

REGRETS RELATED TO FRIENDS

I regret.....

Not finding the time to spend with my family & my friends. Always saying we should or we will get together on a later date. Always finding something more important.

I regret..... Female/28

wasting time and energy on people who didn't deserve my love, loyalty, and friendship... and then not letting go of those feelings when our friendship ended

I regret......

sitting on the sideline and then wondering why I had no friends

Female 28

I regret......

not going next door when my neighbor with 5 kids could have used a hug and support.

female 46

I regret.....

Female, 52

Not connecting w/ my mentally ill friend more before he killed himself

Nearly 1 in 3 friendship regrets involve a friend who died (often unexpectedly).

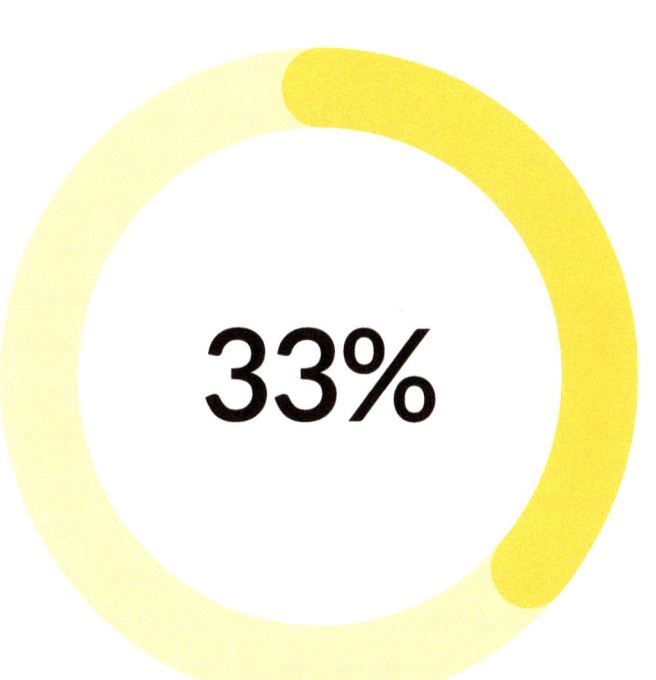

I regret.....
female, 36 years old

not getting on a plane to see my best friend as soon as she was diagnosed with cancer

I regret.....

breaking off friendships for "silly" reasons when they should have meant more than that.

female /33

I regret..... Female 62

Not traveling back to my home town to say goodbye to my best friend who passed away with Brain cancer. She asked me to remember her the way she use to be.

I regret......
not trying harder to mend things with my best friends.

Female, 19

I regret..... Female 51

Not answering a phone call from my friend at 9:53 AM. They hit a tree at 9:58 AM and she Died. along with her 10 yr old & Husband.

Your Turn

Write your regret related to friends:

_____

_____

_____

_____

_____

Go to www.RegretRewrite.com to transform this regret.

REGRETS RELATED TO CAREER & EDUCATION

I regret…..

Female, 50

— Not going to Law School.

I regret.....

not doing a semester abroad or a semester at another university

Female, 44

I regret.....

Not starting a bicycle Touring business with a friend when I was yd

Male 58

I regret..... Female 36

Not making a career change sooner that supports my mental health & work/life balance & connecting w/ my dad before he passed

I regret......

Not having the confidence to charge what I was worth when I started my Business

FEMALE 54

I regret.....

partying like a rockstar in college instead of taking full advantage of the amazing opportunity my parents gave me!

62

I regret......

Not getting my pilots license when I had the chance

Female 42

I regret.....

not taking all of my work vacation days.

female, 60 yrs.

I regret.....

Not taking risks, pushing ~~for~~ advancement/promotions earlier in my career. "I wasn't good enough."

Female 48

1 in 5 career regrets are about playing small (not taking the leap, not speaking up, or not betting on themselves).

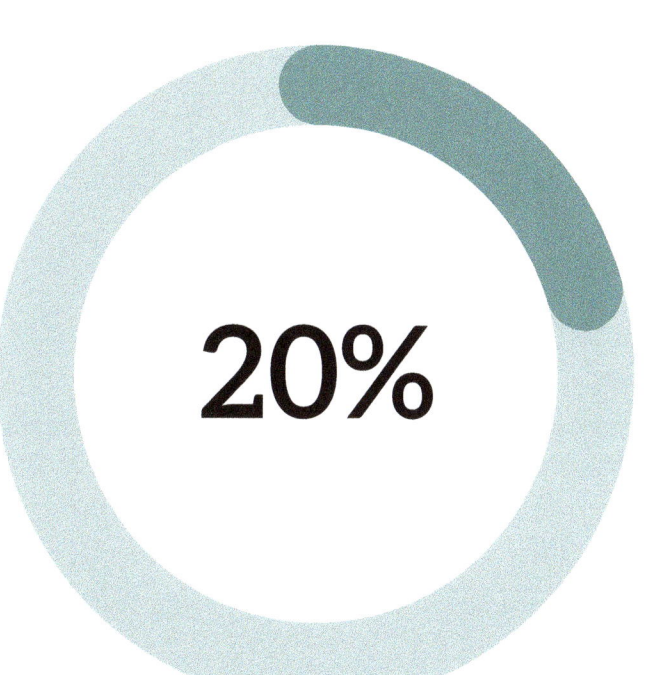

I regret..... Female
Age 39

I regret taking on a 6 figure client that is not in alignment w/ who I am.

I regret...... Female 40

leaving the college I loved because of not knowing at 19 what I wanted to be when I grew up! Gave up experiences to just save money.

I regret.....

working so much! I wanted to be so successful, I forgot what was important and lost my marriage.

I regret.....

Not speaking up to my boss's boss when he asked me about a certain project. I took the blame instead of telling him it was due to my boss's direction.

I regret.....

Not taking that job out of college that would have allowed me to travel around the world.

I regret.....

- Not taking the leap earlier to be my own boss

- letting my career come before my kids

I regret.....

I wish I would've gotten my Masters while still in my 20's. Now I am married with children and saving for their college

Woman - 46

I regret.....

Male 53

Not following through with becoming a policeman or fireman, my 2 dream jobs growing up.

I regret.....

that I hired a friend in my business ... and now we aren't friends.

Female 58

I regret.....

female 57

not going to college because I had a boyfriend I didn't want to lose

Your Turn

Write your regret related to career & education:

_____

_____

_____

_____

Go to www.RegretRewrite.com to transform this regret.

REGRETS RELATED TO FAMILY

I regret.....

Female
Age: 60

I regret allowing my children to see a bad example of marriage thinking I was providing stability.

I regret.....

Allowing my anxiety to pass to my children.

Female: 38

I regret..... Female/Age 32

letting so much time pass since seeing my mom. Not just speaking up and telling her I miss her. Being stubborn and playing "chicken" waiting for her to reach out.

I regret.....

Not going to concerts and events with my mom sooner After learning she'd never gone to any.

Female 128

I regret.....

Playing so much by the rules.

Waiting so long to have kids.

Female 40 y/old

I regret.....

Not being a better sister when my brother needed me, not getting to his beside sooner before he died.

I regret.....

Not paying attention to my grandma when she tried to teach me how to cook

Female - 52

I regret.....

61 F

Not asking my Dad to go on a mission trip the weekend he was killed in a tractor accident and died

I regret......

Having more Children.

I regret......

Female 49

Not having more children so my son has a sibling when I'm gone

I regret.....

ending a pregnancy,

Female 66

I regret......

Speaking ill of my ex-husband when my children were young after we divorced. I should have handled it better.

Female - 65

I regret.....

Female - 37

- Saying no to silly things my daughter asks me to do.

- Not being present more + putting my phone away!

64% of family regrets are about time (moments missed, memories not made, and presence withheld).

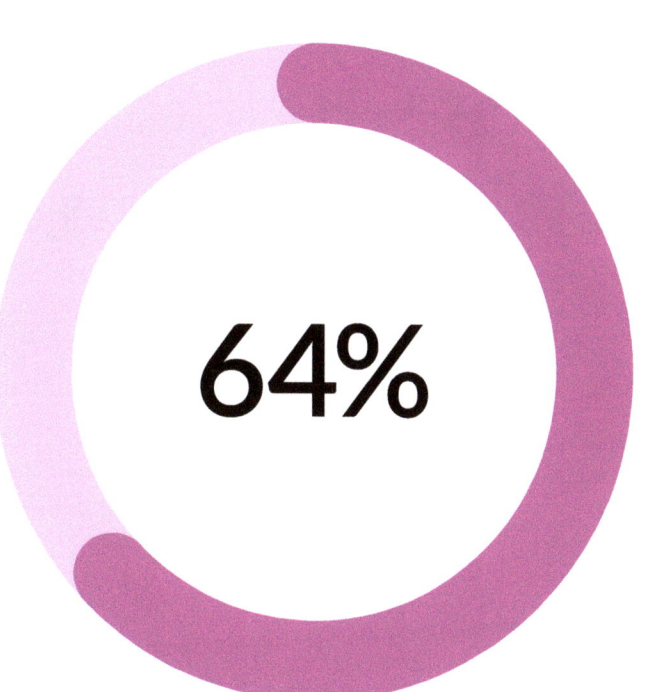

I regret.....

Female / 43

Not being able to get the kids a house til now

I regret.....

Not being honest with my mother about how her actions affected me.

Female, 42

I regret.....

Not being a better daughter to my father whom struggles with Alcoholism
Not being there for him knowing I'm his only child, only person he has to lean on.
Being more of an advocate for my patients than my own father.

Female 32

I regret.....

Not being there more for my little brother (11) when our mom passed away.

Female, 27

I regret.....

Female 54 yo

Not telling the truth as a child when asked about whether a cousin was abusing my sister + I. Couldn't tell my parents "yes" it was happening. Hurt my sister for years.

I regret.....

Female 55

Not *fully* forgiving my father before he passed away.

I regret......

Not being a better mother to my children when we lost their father

I regret.....

Not prying harder when I talked to my mom about her "sounding" different hours before she passed from a heart attack.

Female / 35

Female 42

I regret.....

not having children
and worrying to much
about the "whatifs"
instead of enjoying
the moment!

I regret.....

Not discussing the health dangers of getting the covid shot with my son and the severe health crisis he suffered after it.

Male - 63

I regret.....

Not being more of a mother to my daughter rather than a friend!

Female age 62

I regret.....

buying a car for my son, which he drove to the place where he was killed.

I regret.....

Female, 39

Not visiting my aging grandparents more before they passed <u>and</u> taking more videos of them during visits.

(and overplucking my eyebrows in the '90s)

Your Turn

Write your regret related to family:

_____

_____

_____

_____

Go to www.RegretRewrite.com to transform this regret.

REGRETS RELATED TO SELF

I regret.....

Being afraid to take a chance—
- jumping into the lake
- learning to ski
- smiling back at the cute boy
...

Basically living in fear of trying

Female - 69

I regret.....

F-38

blaming others instead of facing harsh truths about myself

I regret......

Letting things outside my control determine too many things I can control

                                Male 58

I regret......

not giving myself more grace during the hard seasons of my life.

Female, 40

I regret.....

Female 54

letting my weight & fears make me miss events & holding me back from achieving more in life.

I regret.....

letting others influence my emotions and make me second guess my true self.

Female - 57

I regret......

Letting fear of rejection keep me from reaching out to others both personally & professionally.

Female - 49

I regret......

NOT BEING CONFIDENT IN MYSELF, IN MY ACTIONS, AND IN MY EDUCATION TO BE ABLE TO TELL OTHERS NO AND SET THOSE HEALTHY BOUNDARIES.

FEMALE - 39

I regret.....

Setting an example of acceptence in relationships and just "dealing" with the bad for so long.

But worse is now I have to watch my daughter struggle with the same situations with her estranged husband.

It is heart breaking.

Female 48

Self-related regrets make up nearly 35% of all submissions, highlighting how often our greatest struggles are internal.

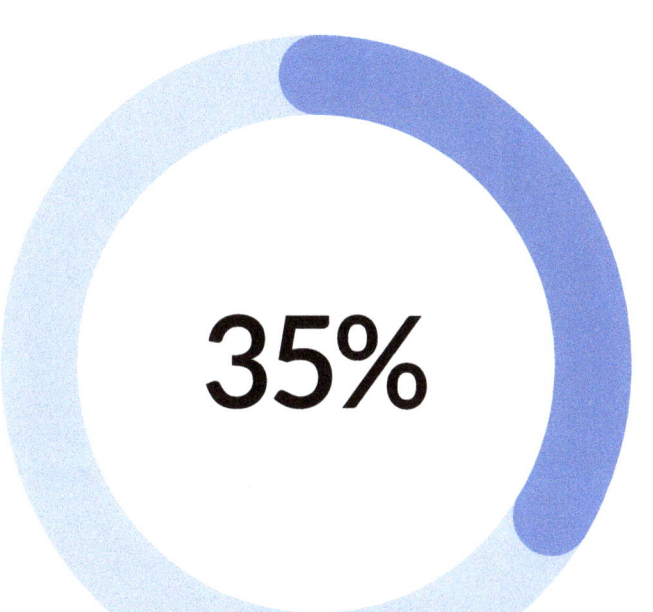

I regret.....

I REGRET NOT IGNORING MY FATHER AND STARTING THAT HEAVY METAL BAND.

MAX, 47

I regret.....

all of the times I wish I spoke up but stayed quiet.

      female 29

I regret......

Not taking more vacations and time for myself

I regret.....

-not being emotionally avalible when important people in my life need me.

-Not living in the moment, Being to time rushed to get tasks donpasted.

Female /31

I regret......

Not listening to those who knew better about a past relationship

I regret......
(Female, 23)

Not taking school seriously when I was younger and not learning how to cook before I moved out on my own.

I regret..... Female - 29 y.o

not coming out sooner & living my true life.

- Finishing my pilot licence.

I regret.....

surrounding myself with people that did not deserve my time or energy.

Female 37

I regret.....

- not taking more pictures of my son
- not eating the last slice of cake
- every yes my mouth gave but my heart said no.

Your Turn

Write your regret related to self:

_____

_____

_____

_____

Go to www.RegretRewrite.com to transform this regret.

REGRETS RELATED TO ROMANTIC PARTNERS

I regret......

Arguing with my husband over stupid things, wasted our presious time together

Gender - female   Age 58

I regret.....
not getting out of a relationship I was not happy in because of the fear of being alone/moving on.

Female 25

I regret.....

not having deeper conversations with my husband. Many missed opportunities for a stronger connection ♡

I regret.....

not finding myself before I got married at way to young of an age ... 22 Didn't experience enough dates to know if I married the right guy.

I regret.....

not leaving a relationship sooner, not leaving a job sooner, doing too much for a doomed relationship and not putting me first.

I regret.....

Female, 33

Not recognizing my husband's addiction earlier.

I regret.....

not going out more on dates when asked, not knowing how truly wonderful I am sooner, and letting people take advantage of my kindness.

female/43

Unlike most categories, romantic partner regrets are split almost evenly between regrets about actions taken (such as staying too long) and actions not taken (like being more supportive).

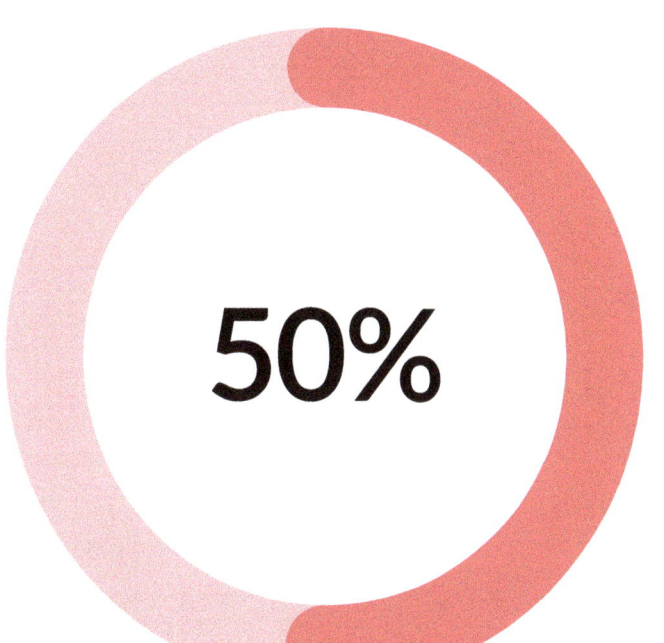

I regret......

Not being As Kind to My Wife As I Am to Others. I interact with

male 62

I regret..... age 55

1) not listening to my gut the night before my wedding ...and walking away
2) not going to church with my mom, when she asked me to before she died
3) not going to see Pink Floyd with my mom in Chicago when I was in high school

I regret.....

Female 67

Marrying who my parents didn't want me to. They were wiser and in the end, they were right.

I regret......

Having an affair instead of forcing my husband & I to confront our distance.

Female 40

I regret...... Male 43

- Dumping Lindsay before prom to go with another girl

- Caring too much what others think

- Not learning Spanish

I regret......

Female 39

I regret dumping all of myself into being a wife and not taking any time for me. Now I feel empty and alone and have no idea who I am.

I regret..... Female 53

Not making the cheesy potato soup for my husband. Fast forward six months - he was diagnosed with cancer and died in 3 weeks.
Make the potato soup

Your Turn

Write your regret related to romantic partners:

_____

_____

_____

_____

Go to www.RegretRewrite.com to transform this regret.

REGRETS RELATED TO MONEY

I regret.....

Female, 38

Not providing more financial stability for my family.

I regret......

Female 31

Living beyond my means because I cared what people thought. Which caused financial stress on my family.

I regret.....

Being money-motivated and not going for the lesser paying job. I feel like I lost out on a few formidable years of my children and valuable time w/ my wife.   Male, 43

I regret..... F, 67

- Not listening to my mom about budgeting
- Not listening to my dad about finance -- saving + investing
- Ignoring the magic of compound interest!
- Not investing sooner

Less than 2% of regrets submitted mention money.

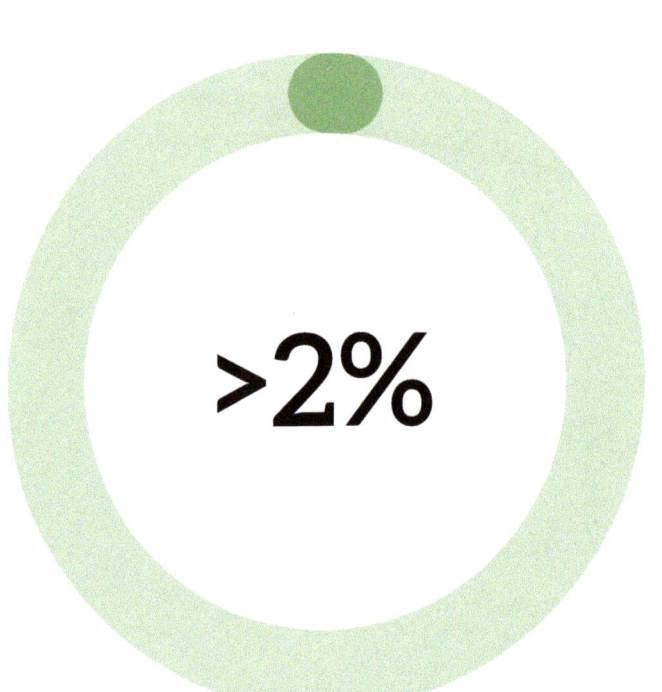

I regret..... —Female 26

moving back home too soon (post grad) instead of trying harder to make it on my own. I only gave myself 2 years and I was so close to becoming truly financially independent but I let fear stop me. But it's still not too late :)

I regret..... –40–female

~~buy~~ buying a house that was at the top end of my budget. When something came up with the house, I had to take on a second job, which took me away from my family.

I regret.....

Female - 50

Not setting up our family finances for success that I ~~~ could quit my job and watch my grandkids full-time at this point of my life.

I regret......

Female 54

waiting to take fabulous trips until we have enough money saved.

Your Turn

Write your regret related to money:

_____

_____

_____

_____

Go to www.RegretRewrite.com to transform this regret.

REGRETS RELATED TO HEALTH

I regret.....

all of the times that i used food for emotional support and comfort.

I regret.....

not paying attention to my health (mostly diet and exercise) when I was younger because I am paying the price for bad habits now.

~~~~~~~~~~ Female 47

I regret.....

Letting my weight problem rule my life and stop me from trying to find my soul mate.

I regret......

Waiting so long to take medication for anxiety

female | 27

I regret.....

① ~~I regret not~~ not prioritizing my health (physical & mental) earlier in my life and career.

② not forgiving my father earlier for cheating on my mom & family. He got ill w/ early onset alzheimers a few years later & passed

ⓐ lele - I missed so many years w/ my Dad.

85% of health regrets are about delay (waiting too long to take action, get help, or make changes).

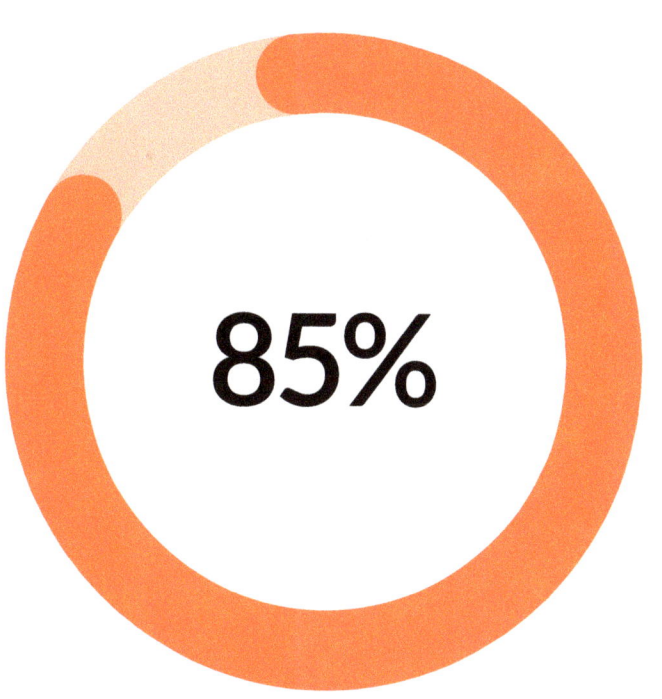

I regret......

Female / 42 years

Not getting the mole on my back removed sooner.

Not going into the Peace Corp or missionary work after college.

I regret.....

7-48

gaining back weight I worked hard to lose.

I regret.....

Not staying committed to my health after getting a 2nd chance @ it

female, 41

Your Turn

Write your regret related to health:

_____

_____

_____

_____

Go to www.RegretRewrite.com to transform this regret.

REGRETS RELATED TO MISCELLANEOUS MOMENTS

I regret.....

female, Age 37

not saying "yes" to more opportunites for growth, for fun, for Love ♡

I regret.....

not keeping my dog who I loved so much when I got divorced.

Female
44

I regret.....

Not playing volleyball in college and ~~other~~ missing out on travel experiences when I was young because I thought it seemed too expensive.

      Female, 43

I regret.....

Female 55

Not wearing sexy clothes while I had the body and youth to show it off properly!

I regret.....

- taking people for granted
- not treating subordinates nicer
- not seeing/visiting all MLB stadiums
- not eating veggies

Male
Age 55

I regret.....

- Not ever living anywhere outside of Il.

- Not being consistent w/ self care

- Not being true to me

- loosing my footing after my husband passed

I regret......

Not visiting the World Trade Center in 2000 when I had the chance

Age 39

I regret.....

Age 59, female

Believing EVERYTHING I was taught throughout my Catholic education (elementary – H.S.). I missed out on a lot of good, healthy fun & experiences.

64% of all regrets are rooted in *inaction* in the things people *wished* they'd done but didn't.

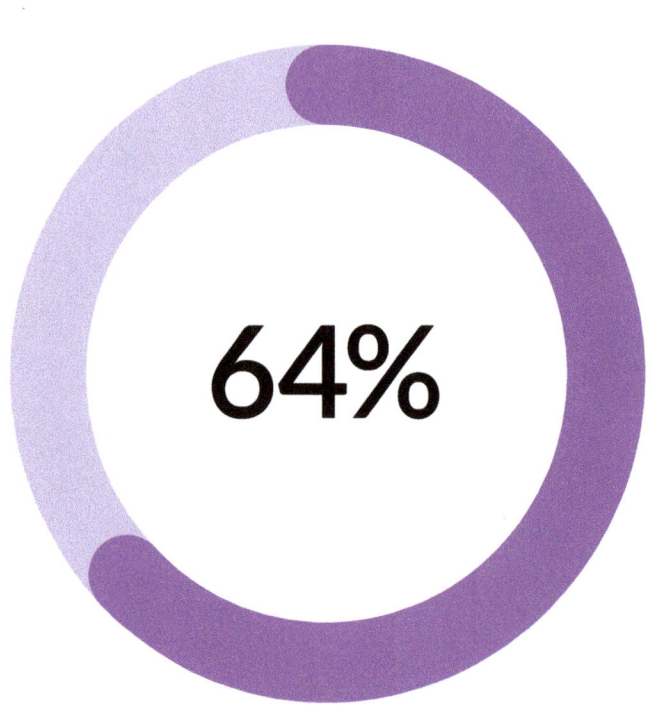

I regret.....

Spending too many years using alcohol as my cure for social anxiety. I lost a lot of great nights and potential relationships.

Male - 41 years

I regret.....

- not pursuing a diff. career path.
- not hugging my dad one last time.
- wasting so much time on social media.
- distancing myself from a cousin in addiction + losing her suddenly.

I regret......

not addressing the priest who abused me.

Male 62

I regret.....

not spending more time with my grandparents when I had the chance.

not spending time w/ my kids when I'm too tired.

Not reporting my abuser so it didn't happen to others.

I regret.....

not going to Hawaii when I had the chance at age 20.

P.S. I've yet to go and I'm almost 50.

I regret.....

Not helping more of the homeless people on the side of the road.

Female / 32

I regret.....

Making the decision to stop for food which led to a DUI

Male, 51

I regret.....

1. Not going to Radford College & becoming a NP
2. Not going on a mission trip
3. Not having 1 more child
4. Not starting a retirement savings sooner
5. Not staying in Ops role
6. Selling my last house
7. Moving to VA Beach
8. Not spending more time with my Dad, Step Dad, Grandaddy & Nanny before they passed

9) Gaining ALL of my weight back
10) Trying to please everyone & losing myself & what I want
11) Not learning to Tango
12) Not learning to play Violin
13) Not opening my own business
14) Not taking a girls trip to Ireland
15) Not going into Holistic Medicine
16) not finishing Massage Therapy School

Gender Female   Age 54

I regret.....

Missing opportunities to say, "I love you."

Female 53

Your Turn

Write your regret related to miscellaneous moments:

_____

_____

_____

_____

Go to www.RegretRewrite.com to transform this regret.

REGRET REWRITE

By now, you've seen the raw, honest truth: regret lives inside all of us. Some regrets make us smile. Others leave a lump in our throat. But here's the good news—regret doesn't have to be where the story ends.

We can't change the past. But we can change what we do next. Regret isn't a stop sign—it's a spotlight, showing you exactly where your heart is asking for more. More courage. More connection. More life.

If something stirred inside you as you read these regrets—your own regrets whispered back—that's not a coincidence. That's your invitation.

Here are a few simple ways to start rewriting the story:

- ✓ Call the person you've been meaning to reconnect with.
- ✓ Book the trip—even if it's small.
- ✓ Apologize, forgive, or express gratitude—before it feels "too late."
- ✓ Take the class, write the book, make the bold move.
- ✓ Start today—even if it's messy. Especially if it's messy.
- ✓ Write a letter to someone you've lost—say the things left unsaid.
- ✓ Get quiet. Reflect. Then act.

Even the smallest step forward can help release what's been weighing you down.

And if you're ready for something more personal… you don't have to do this alone. Go here:

to access your own private Regret Rewrite session. You'll get customized feedback, tailored insights, and next steps to help you move forward—all based on your specific regret.

It's time to release the past and fuel your future.

Ready to stop putting your goals on the back burner?

If you've been inspired by what's inside these pages… just imagine what's possible when you have personal support to make bold moves, release regret, and create your next chapter—with no limits and no apologies.

I work with women leaders to make bold moves so they can live with no regrets and no limits.

Whether it's through private coaching, transformational programs, or live experiences, if you're ready to take the next step, I'm here to guide you.

Scan the QR code to explore upcoming programs and resources to fuel your future.

Your next chapter starts now.

Bring an unforgettable, transformational experience to your audience.

As a dynamic speaker and creator of the Regret Release Method, I've guided thousands of people to let go of what's been holding them back—so they can lead with courage, clarity, and confidence.

My keynotes and workshops are thought-provoking, interactive, and refreshingly real—blending storytelling, audience engagement, and actionable tools to spark lasting change.

From conferences and corporate events to leadership retreats, I bring energy, authenticity, and tangible results.

Scan the QR code to learn more about my topics, watch video clips, and schedule a call to see if I'm a fit for your event.

Let's create a no-regrets experience for your audience.

ACKNOWLEDGMENTS

This book is the culmination of so many people and experiences and wonderful "coincidences" that I can't begin to tally.

To my amazing book team—Susan Friedmann and Catherine Williams—you helped me stay on course and literally bring this idea to life.

To my coach, mentor, friend, and sister from another mister, Michelle Villalobos—you've always seen the best in me and I am eternally grateful. You've helped me evolve and grow and heal and own my true gifts and mission.

To my dear friends Lisa Corrado, Marvin Acuna, and Kimberly Faith Rayburn, who have all held space while I cried, encouraged me when I felt lost, and laughed until we cried—I treasure every moment and look forward to many more.

To my friend and amazing support, Kellie Coombes—your support and steadfast belief helps me turn on more lights than I ever thought possible (and have fun in the process!)

And to my clients, audiences, colleagues and everyone in my life… whether we've connected for moments or years, I treasure every connection and sincerely hope you know I love you.

I regret.....

Absolutely NOTHING!

Male 53

www.ingramcontent.com/pod-product-compliance
Lightning Source LLC
Chambersburg PA
CBHW050803220426
43209CB00089BA/1677